EXCEL
VLOOKUP
CHAMPION

HENRY E. MEJIA

EXCEL VLOOKUP CHAMPION

Copyright © 2018 HENRY E. MEJIA

ISBN-13: 978-1720951117
ISBN-10: 172095111X

DEDICATION

To my parents, who have taught me that life is about overcoming obstacles and enjoying it.

CONTENTS

ACKNOWLEDGMENTS

I would like to thank all those who supported me throughout the creation of this book, either with words of encouragement or with ideas to improve it.

INTRODUCTION

Welcome to a new Excel Champions Series book!

What characterizes this series of written courses is that you will learn while you practice because they are full of exercises, examples explained step by step, and real life applicable situations. I also include Excel files so you can practice all the book exercises at home. In fact, you will have 30 exercises to practice with.

Did you know that being an Excel Champion increases your chances of getting promotions and better jobs? If you do not believe me, continue reading.

In fact it is very simple to explain: The person who is an Excel Champion can complete the work better and investing less time in front of the computer, as a result has more time available to tackle other activities that need attention and achieve a better outcome at the end of the day.

I know this because I have personally experienced it. Thanks to Excel I was able to get a better job and also thanks to Excel I was promoted. In case you're thinking about it, it was not in any Business Intelligence department nor in Corporate Finance (where Excel is extremely indispensable), it was in the Accounting department and the Sales department. Why did my bosses give such importance to Excel knowledge?

Actually Excel is used in almost any department of any company, private or government. Wherever you work, being an Excel Champion will give you a clear advantage over your other co-workers and will put you in a position to move up or look for a better place.

HOW CAN THIS BOOK HELP YOU BECOME AN EXCEL VLOOKUP CHAMPION?

To be an Excel Champion it is necessary that you master several tools and formulas. In this book I will teach you in detail and step by step the VLOOKUP formula

VLOOKUP is a search formula that, if used in the right way, helps drastically reduce the time you use in front of the computer when working with databases.

Let me tell you a story, a person who had the position of Warehouse Coordinator in a retail company didn't use VLOOKUP to build a monthly report of merchandise shipments. How much time did he spend every month? 3 hours.

One day that person asked me if there was any faster way (I'm glad he asked!) And I taught him how to use VLOOKUP in a very basic way. How much time did use later in the same report? 45 minutes! In case you haven't noticed, that's 4 times faster. Not bad for a simple formula, don't you think?

That happens with a basic domain of VLOOKUP, but when you have giant databases and you are a VLOOKUP Champion you can expect even better results.

HOW CAN THIS BOOK HELP YOU TO HAVE A BETTER LIFE?

Can you imagine being able to leave the office at 5pm almost everyday? Can you imagine being able to have most of the reports in order and ready without delays? What would you do if that happened? Would you go running, to the gym, to dinner with your family, to the movies, would you learn to play a musical instrument?

All that is possible if you manage to become an Excel Champion. Excel can do the heavy lifting of calculating and finding data for you. The repetitive tasks that you do can be automated by creating templates. In some cases Excel can even make decisions for you if you organize your requirements beforehand.

Less time in front of the computer means more time for important tasks of your work and more time for important people like your family.

SO, WHAT WILL I LEARN EXACTLY?

In a few words, you will learn to use VLOOKUP in many different ways in your job or business. VLOOKUP is a tool, think of it as a hammer, that is also a tool. Both can be used for different situations. Here you will learn to use VLOOKUP in different situations of real life so that none of them take you by surprise.

You will learn in a practical and straightforward way, with this course full of exercises and examples. You can also use the *.xlsx* files to practice.

You will learn quickly and in an easy to understand way. You can achieve a basic level from the first 3 chapters of the book, while in the following chapters you can become an Excel VLOOKUP Champion and be the best in your workplace using this powerful tool.

I want to thank you for allowing me to share this knowledge with you. I sincerely hope that you apply everything you learn and that you get the positive results in your job or business.

It's time for you to start your journey as an Excel Vlookup Champion.

GET YOUR 30 PRACTICE SPREADSHEETS (.XLSX)

Before starting Chapter 1 I recommend you get your 30 practice spreadsheets. To get them immediately just **Scan this QR Code or go directly to https://bit.ly/hemejia2 and follow the instructions**

If for any reason both the QR Code and the Link don't work, send an email to ems.online.empire@gmail.com saying: **"Hello, I bought your book EXCEL VLOOKUP CHAMPION and I need the 30 practice spreadsheets"**

Now, it is time to start Chapter 1. Let's go!

CHAPTER 1:

WHAT IS VLOOKUP AND WHICH ARE ITS BENEFITS?

WHAT IS A FUNCTION?

An Excel function is a tool used to make calculations, searches, changes or logical reasoning with the data you provide, with the objective of returning a result.

Functions (or formulas) always start with the sign of =

Every time you try to write a function you must select the cell and start with a =

In a simple way, using functions saves you the hard work and it is Excel who works hard to give you the result you are looking for. Less work for you and less time in the office!

"Using functions (formulas) saves you a lot of hard work."

Excel is one of the most powerful software, it has many functions and many tools, and in this book you will learn one of the most useful: VLOOKUP

WHAT IS VLOOKUP?

Vlookup is one of the most useful Excel functions. You can use it in different ways but **basically it helps you find information within a giant amount of data.**

IMPORTANT NOTE:

VLOOKUP is the formula in English.

If you use Excel in Spanish, the formula works the same, with the only difference that VLOOKUP in Spanish is called BUSCARV.

You only need to enter in the formula =BUSCARV instead of =VLOOKUP and voila, everything else remains the same.

Sometimes, you need to find the exact price (or any other information) of a certain Product ID, but you have many products. What someone who is not a Vlookup Champion does is to search the price of each product in their database and copy it manually, one by one. What a waste of time! What a Vlookup Champion does is to use the formula to get the right prices from the database and in 30 seconds all the prices along with their respective Product ID are in place, with zero errors.

> **"If you have a list of names or numbers and you need to relate it to other data, Vlookup helps you find that information in a database, in just a few seconds and without errors."**

It is possible that you have a list of students, clients, stores, employees, vehicles, invoices, and you need to place certain information next to them without errors to be able to do an analysis with or without graphs, VLOOKUP helps you to do that in a matter of seconds.

EXAMPLE:

Imagine that you have this daily sales table, and you need to fill out the product description and the employee who sold it:

PRODUCT ID	EMPLOYEE ID	PRODUCT DESCRIPTION	EMPLOYEE NAME
4	111		
5	110		
1	110		
3	113		
1	112		
1	111		
2	111		

It would take you easily 3 or 4 minutes to fill it out manually and with the risk of having errors, and there are only 7 sales. When you face hundreds of sales you can end up with some complications. But if you have previously a "master table" where you have the list of all the product IDs and their descriptions **(that "master table" is called Database** and it is usually obtained from the ERP System of the business) you can use Vlookup and within 15 seconds you will have the product descriptions in order. Another 15 seconds and you would have the names of the employees too.

> **"When you are a Vlookup Champion you need only 1 minute to search and write what used to take you 10 minutes without Vlookup"**

THE BENEFITS OF USING VLOOKUP AS A CHAMPION

Well, it's obvious that knowing how to use Vlookup doesn't make you look sexier in the office (although sometimes it does) but it has many other benefits:

• You can save a lot of time of searching and filling spreadsheets with information of databases. That is, you have more chances to leave the office early and have done what they ask.

• Most of the time you will have zero errors, and when you have one you can immediately notice it. Never again give incorrect information to the boss. Avoid ending up the day with a long face.

• Vlookup makes it easy for you to learn other Excel functions. Combining functions is one way to get the best out of Excel, and using Vlookup as a Champion is a great start to achieve that.

• You can spend more time analyzing the information and searching ways to improve your work. How on earth can you analyze the information if you use hours to obtain it and organize it? By the time you finish you are tired, stressed and hungry! It's better to use VLOOKUP.

Now that you understand the benefits of being a Vlookup Champion, you will be more motivated to be one. In the next chapter you will learn the parts that make up the Vlookup function quickly and easily. Once you understand the structure and its parts you will begin with the exercises.

QUICK CHAPTER SUMMARY

- Vlookup will save you time and prevent you from making mistakes.
- Vlookup will allow you to analyze more information and make better decisions in your job or business

CHAPTER 2:

THE VLOOKUP STRUCTURE

WHAT IS A DATABASE?

A database is an organized set of data, usually in the form of a table, which can be a giant one and contain thousands of rows of information (literally thousands).

Why is it important? **Because VLOOKUP gathers the information from the Database you pick**. That's right, without a database, Vlookup can't help you get out of the office early.

Remember the Image of chapter 1, where you have to write the product description and the employee name, you will get that data from one or more of these databases:

	F	G
1		PRODUCTS
2	**ID**	**DESCRIPTION**
3	1	Shirt
4	2	Cell Phone
5	3	TV
6	4	Jeans
7	5	Watch
8	6	Dinner Table
9	7	Home Theater

	I	J
1		EMPLOYEES
2	**ID**	**NAME**
3	110	John Maxwell
4	111	Robert Kiyosaki
5	112	Tim Ferris
6	113	Mark Zuckemberg
7	114	Henry Ford
8	115	Elon Musk
9	116	Bill Gates

The previous images show two databases from where you get the information that Vlookup needs to work, in this case they are small databases and don't represent many problems, but what would you do if the company has more than 100 different products or more than 100 different employees? What would you do if they asked you to fill 100 sales a day? You need to use Vlookup to get all the information quickly.

> ## "Databases feed the Vlookup function"

THE 4 PARTS OF VLOOKUP, THE ARGUMENTS

Vlookup has four parts in its formula and are known as arguments or parameters. So every time I say "arguments" or "parameters" you know I'm talking about the parts of the formula.

> ## How is the formula inserted in Excel?
>
> ## Double click on the cell where you want to insert it

That is the "Syntax" of Vlookup. Syntax is a very sophisticated word to refer to the Structure or the Formula, so I better keep calling it the "Structure", but if someone else asks you "What is the Vlookup SYNTAX?" you will know the answer.

You will find the four arguments inside the parentheses separated by a comma (,) and you need to know them very well. I'll explain them one by one.

LOOKUP VALUE (1ST ARGUMENT)

Lookup value is the reference value, the value on which the outcome of the formula depends. If you change the Lookup Value, the outcome changes. You can understand it as the anchor value. The formula will read the Lookup value, it will look it up within the database and return the result that matches.

Visually, imagine that you are asked to fill in the product descriptions, so you decide to write the VLOOKUP formula in cell C3 to start:

	A	B	C	D	E	F	G
1			DAILY SALES				PRODUCTS
2	PRODUCT ID	EMPLOYEE ID	PRODUCT DESCRIPTION	EMPLOYEE NAME		ID	DESCRIPTION
3	4	111				1	Shirt
4	5	110				2	Cell Phone
5	1	110				3	TV
6	3	113				4	Jeans
7	1	112				5	Watch
8	1	111				6	Dinner Table
9	2	111				7	Home Theater

Step 1: Notice that on the right side you have a very small database called "Products" that has the IDs and descriptions.

Step 2: Observe that in your "Daily Sales" table you have the same Product ID that the database has, so you can relate them.

Step 3: Use the Product ID of your daily sales table as the Lookup Value, that is cell A3. ID "4" will be the reference value you will use this time.

And the formula is going to start like this:

=VLOOKUP(A3, **Table array, Column index num, Range Lookup)**

> ## Tip:
>
> ### Whenever you look for the Vlookup Value ask yourself "What is my reference value?" Or "What value can I use that is also in the database?"

We have the first argument explained! Lets go to the second one.

TABLE ARRAY (2nd ARGUMENT)

Table array is the range where Vlookup will search for information, to make it easier to understand, **it is the set of cells where the database is located.**

It is expressed in matrix form, for example: A Range of A1:C5 means that it spans from cells A1 to A5, from B1 to B5 and from C1 to C5, a total of 15 cells are in this "range". The first part of the range (A1 in the example) is the cell in the upper left corner of the range, and the second part of the range (C5) is the cell in the lower right corner of the range.

Lets see again the image.

	A	B	C	D	E	F	G
1			DAILY SALES				PRODUCTS
2	PRODUCT ID	EMPLOYEE ID	PRODUCT DESCRIPTION	EMPLOYEE NAME		ID	DESCRIPTION
3	4	111				1	Shirt
4	5	110				2	Cell Phone
5	1	110				3	TV
6	3	113				4	Jeans
7	1	112				5	Watch
8	1	111				6	Dinner Table
9	2	111				7	Home Theater

Step 1: Find the database. In image 5 it is in a box (range F2: G9)

Step 2: The range will cover the entire database, **therefore our Table Array would be F2: G9.** Why? Well, because F2 is the upper left corner of the range, and G9 is the lower right corner of the range.

The formula now looks like this:

=VLOOKUP(A3,F2:G9, **Column index num, Range Lookup)**

Tip:

To find the Table Array, ask: "In which range of cells is my database located?"

COLUMN INDEX NUMBER (3RD ARGUMENT)

It is the number of the column, inside your Table Array, where the result that you want to obtain as a result is found. In the image you can see the result you want (Product Description) is in the 2nd column of the Table Array.

Step 1: Remember that the Table Array is the range F2: G9.

Step 2: The first column of the Table Array should ALWAYS be where the Lookup Value will be searched. If your Lookup Value is a product ID, the first Column of your Table

Array must be the column of the Product IDs.

Step 3: Lets count the columns, if F is column one, G is column 2, and if you want the results of G (Product descriptions) then your Column Index Number is 2!

The formula now looks like this:

=VLOOKUP(A3,F2:G9,2, **Range Lookup)**

Tip:

To find the Column Index Number ask:
"In which column, within my database, is
the result I want?"

RANGE LOOKUP (4TH ARGUMENT)

The fourth argument is OPTIONAL and allows you to describe if you want Vlookup to look for the Exact or Approximate reference value. If you decide Exact, the Lookup Value must be written exactly the same form in the database. If you decide approximate, the formula will return the value that is closest to your Lookup Value, but there may be errors.

EXACT: write "FALSE" o "0"

APPROXIMATE: write "TRUE" o "1"

To avoid getting wrong information, I always use the exact form. In very few occasions I had used the approximate coincidence, therefore in this book we will use the exact one.

When you complete the formula with the Exact Match Range Lookup =VLOOKUP(A3,F2:G9,2,0) you get the expected outcome, "Jeans" is the Product Description with ID 4.

	A	B	C	D	E	F	G
1			DAILY SALES				PRODUCTS
2	PRODUCT ID	EMPLOYEE ID	PRODUCT DESCRIPTION	EMPLOYEE NAME		ID	DESCRIPTION
3	4	111	Jeans			1	Shirt
4	5	110				2	Cell Phone
5	1	110				3	TV
6	3	113				4	Jeans
7	1	112				5	Watch
8	1	111				6	Dinner Table
9	7	111				7	Home Theater

Congratulations, now you understand the 4 arguments of Vlookup! In the next chapter you will begin your exercises to become an Excel Vlookup Champion.

4 THINGS YOU NEED TO REMEMBER DURING YOUR TRAINING AS A VLOOKUP CHAMPION

1) VLOOKUP SEARCHES FROM LEFT TO RIGHT

The first column you select in your Table Array is where Vlookup will look for the Lookup Value (reference value), because Vlookup searches from left to right, never from right to left.

If your reference value is a product ID, **your Table Array should be the one on**

columns F and G, because the ID is in the first column (F) and will return any result to the right of F. If you choose the columns "I" and "J" as a Table Array, the formula will not work because Vlookup will search on the first column (I) for the product ID and will not find it.

Sometimes your database (Table Array) does not have the reference value in its first column (in this case the product ID), as in the following image:

Note that the Database has 4 columns: Stock, Category, ID and Description.

You can't choose the 4 columns as Table Array, **you need your first column of the Table Array to contain the Product ID you are looking for.** Your Table Array should be the H2: I9 range.

Remember:

Vlookup looks for your Lookup Value in the first column of your Table Array, and then returns any result you want, as long as it is on the RIGHT of its first column (e.g. column 2, 3, 10, 20, etc.)

---

2) VLOOKUP FINDS THE FIRST RESULT

Imagine for a moment that in the previous image, within your database, two products have the same ID, for example imagine that ID 4 have "Jeans" and "Home Theater". **Vlookup will always show the first result that matches the Lookup Value**, in this case 4 finds "Jeans".

There are ways to overcome the problem of repeated values in the list you are trying to fill, however the database must have 100% correct information for Vlookup to do its job.

3) VLOOKUP DOESN'T DISTINGUISH CAPITAL LETTERS

If the Lookup Value contains letters, it will not matter if they are written in uppercase or lowercase. Jeans will mean the same as JEANS for Vlookup.

4) VLOOKUP AUTOMATICALLY USES EXACT COINCIDENCE

If you choose to skip the optional fourth argument, Range Lookup will automatically use the EXACT match mode.

QUICK CHAPTER SUMMARY:

- Databases feed the Vlookup function
- There are four arguments (parts) within the function. Three are mandatory and the fourth is optional.
- Lookup Value is the reference value.

- Table Array is the range of the database.

- Column Index Number is the column number where the result you want is located.

- Range Lookup is optional and is almost always used as Exact Match (0)

Four important features must be remembered from the Vlookup function.

CHAPTER 3:

BEGINNING TO BECOME A VLOOKUP CHAMPION

Now that you know the 4 arguments of Vlookup you can start with the exercises. Always remember the following: Practice makes the master. That's why the most important thing is that you practice with the files that are included in this book.

EXERCISE (Open file named chapter3ex1.xlsx)

Following the table in the previous chapter, you have the following task. You need to find the product description for ALL daily sales. The fastest way is to use Vlookup and we will solve this exercise together, step-by-step.

	A	B	C	D	E	F	G
1			DAILY SALES				PRODUCTS
2	EMPLOYEE ID	PRODUCT ID	EMPLOYEE NAME	PRODUCT DESCRIPTION		ID	DESCRIPTION
3	111	4	Mercedez Uyehara			1	Shirt
4	110	5	Refugia Sawicki			2	Cell Phone
5	110	1	Refugia Sawicki			3	TV
6	113	3	Janel Joplin			4	Jeans
7	112	1	Lavenia Ebner			5	Watch
8	111	1	Mercedez Uyehara			6	Dinner Table
9	111	2	Mercedez Uyehara			7	Home Theater

Step 1: Identify which cells you must fill. In this exercise you need to fill the product description cells.

Step 2: Identify in which cell you want the result, that is where you must place the first formula. In this case we will start with cell D3, which is the first cell of product description that you must fill.

Step 3: Double click on cell D3 and start writing the formula:

= VLOOKUP(

Step 4: It's time for you to write the 4 arguments, each argument separated by a comma (,)

Step 4.1: "What value can I use that is also in the database?" **The Product ID**, that is, B3

TIP:

Right after writing =VLOOKUP(You can write B3 inside the formula. You can also click on cell B3, both ways add the cell to the formula.

Step 4.2: "In which range of cells is my database?" F2:G9. You can write it or select the range by clicking and dragging the cursor.

Step 4.3: "In which column, within my database, is the result I want?" Column G. If F is column 1 of your database, then G is column 2. You must write the number 2 in the third argument.

Step 4.4: Do I want an exact result? Yes, then you write 0 or FALSE within the fourth argument.

The formula is
= VLOOKUP(B3,F2:G9,2,0) **and shows**

the result "Jeans"

	A	B	C	D	E	F	G
1			DAILY SALES				PRODUCTS
2	EMPLOYEE ID	PRODUCT ID	EMPLOYEE NAME	PRODUCT DESCRIPTION		ID	DESCRIPTION
3	111	4	Mercedez Uyehara	Jeans		1	Shirt
4	110	5	Refugia Sawicki			2	Cell Phone
5	110	1	Refugia Sawicki			3	TV
6	113	3	Janel Joplin			4	Jeans
7	112	1	Lavenia Ebner			5	Watch
8	111	1	Mercedez Uyehara			6	Dinner Table
9	111	2	Mercedez Uyehara			7	Home Theater

Congratulations! You have your first correct result.

Now you need to add the other results and to avoid writing the formula multiple times, it is easier to **"drag" the formula to the following cells**. That's what step 5 is for.

Step 5: Step 5 will be a bit long because I have to explain additional information. Now that you need to drag the formula to get the result of cells D4 to D9 you will face a small obstacle. Do the following:

Step 5.1: Click on cell D3 and then double click on the lower right corner of the cell. Another option is to click on the lower right corner and without releasing the click drag the cursor down. This will cause the VLOOKUP formula to be repeated in the following cells. **However, you can see #N/A errors.**

	A	B	C	D	E	F	G
1			DAILY SALES				PRODUCTS
2	EMPLOYEE ID	PRODUCT ID	EMPLOYEE NAME	PRODUCT DESCRIPTION		ID	DESCRIPTION
3	111	4	Mercedez Uyehara	Jeans		1	Shirt
4	110	5	Refugia Sawicki	Watch		2	Cell Phone
5	110	1	Refugia Sawicki	#N/A		3	TV
6	113	3	Janel Joplin	TV		4	Jeans
7	112	1	Lavenia Ebner	#N/A		5	Watch
8	111	1	Mercedez Uyehara	#N/A		6	Dinner Table
9	111	2	Mercedez Uyehara	#N/A		7	Home Theater

Why do #N/A errors arise?

The #N/A error appears when the formula can not find the Lookup Value inside the Table Array. In simple words, the formula does not find the value you are looking for in the database.

Step 5.2: Check the formula to find the error. By double clicking on the cell that shows #N/A you can find the errors visually.

To modify any formula you can double click on the cell you want to modify and you can see the formula inside the cell.

In addition you can visualize the arguments with different colors, making it easier to find any error and fix it.

Notice that each argument **has a color assigned and shows the cells with that same color.** In this way you can identify easily and quickly the error of your formula.

	A	B	C	D	E	F	G
1			DAILY SALES				PRODUCTS
2	EMPLOYEE ID	PRODUCT ID	EMPLOYEE NAME	PRODUCT DESCRIPTION		ID	DESCRIPTION
3	111	4	Mercedez Uyehara	Jeans		1	Shirt
4	110	5	Refugia Sawicki	Watch		2	Cell Phone
5	110	1	Refugia Sawic	=VLOOKUP(B5,F4:G11,2,0)		3	TV
6	113	3	Janel Joplin	TV		4	Jeans
7	112	1	Lavenia Ebner	#N/A		5	Watch
8	111	1	Mercedez Uyehara	#N/A		6	Dinner Table
9	111	2	Mercedez Uyehara	#N/A		7	Home Theater
10							
11							

	A	B	C	D	E	F	G
1			DAILY SALES				PRODUCTS
2	EMPLOYEE ID	PRODUCT ID	EMPLOYEE NAME	PRODUCT DESCRIPTION		ID	DESCRIPTION
3	111	4	Mercedez Uyehara	Jeans		1	Shirt
4	110	5	Refugia Sawicki	Watch		2	Cell Phone
5	110	1	Refugia Sawicki	#N/A		3	TV
6	113	3	Janel Joplin	TV		4	Jeans
7	112	1	Lavenia Ebner	=VLOOKUP(B7,F6:G13,2,0)		5	Watch
8	111	1	Mercedez Uyehara	#N/A		6	Dinner Table
9	111	2	Mercedez Uyehara	#N/A		7	Home Theater
10							
11							
12							
13							

Note that the Lookup Value was "moved away". The formula in D3 has its Lookup Value in B1, the formula in D5 has its Lookup Value in B5, and that is correct. **But if you look in more detail, the Table Array was also moved away!** Your database is not immobilized, fixed, or whatever you want to call it, and that causes the #N/A error. **You must immobilize your database.**

> **How is any cell or range "fixed" or "immobilized" within a formula?**
>
> **With absolute references, adding dollar signs to the formula.**
>
> **$F$4 is an example of absolute reference**

$F$4 in a formula is an absolute reference, while **F4** is a relative reference. If you use $F$4 in your formula, you can copy it and paste it anywhere, and your formula will still refer to cell F4, because you "fixed" it. In the exercise you must "fix" your Table Array.

Step 5.3: Fix or "inmovilze" your Table Array range.

Go back to the beginning, to your formula in D3 which was: **=VLOOKUP(B3,F2:G9,2,0)**

You need to change it to: *=VLOOKUP(B3,$F$2:$G$9,2,0)* to immobilize your database within the formula. Dollar signs are added to both F2 and G9 because they are the data that make up the range.

Option 1 to add absolute reference: Double click on cell D3 and modify the formula manually

Option 2 to add absolute reference: Double click in cell D3, click in the middle of F2 (in the formula) and; if you use Windows press F4, if you use Macbook press Cmd + T. That will automatically add the absolute reference to F2. Do the same to add the absolute reference to G9.

Your formula in D3 should look like this:

=VLOOKUP(B3,$F$2:$G$9,2,0)

	A	B	C	D	E	F	G
1			DAILY SALES				PRODUCTS
2	EMPLOYEE ID	PRODUCT ID	EMPLOYEE NAME	PRODUCT DESCRIPTION		ID	DESCRIPTION
3	111	4	Mercedez Uye	=VLOOKUP(B3,$F$2:$G$9,2,0)		1	Shirt
4	110	5	Refugia Sawicki	Watch		2	Cell Phone
5	110	1	Refugia Sawicki	Shirt		3	TV
6	113	3	Janel Joplin	TV		4	Jeans
7	112	1	Lavenia Ebner	Shirt		5	Watch
8	111	1	Mercedez Uyehara	Shirt		6	Dinner Table
9	111	2	Mercedez Uyehara	Cell Phone		7	Home Theater

Step 5.4: Drag the formula and now you will not get any error. Click on D3, click on the lower right corner and without releasing the click drag the cursor from D3 to D9.

If you analyze the formulas in all the cells you can see that the Table Array stays exactly in the same static range, always referring to the database that you indicated.

	A	B	C	D	E	F	G
1			DAILY SALES				PRODUCTS
2	EMPLOYEE ID	PRODUCT ID	EMPLOYEE NAME	PRODUCT DESCRIPTION		ID	DESCRIPTION
3	111	4	Mercedez Uyehara	Jeans		1	Shirt
4	110	5	Refugia Sawicki	Watch		2	Cell Phone
5	110	1	Refugia Sawicki	Shirt		3	TV
6	113	3	Janel Joplin	TV		4	Jeans
7	112	1	Lavenia Ebner	=VLOOKUP(B7,$F$2:$G$9,2,0)		5	Watch
8	111	1	Mercedez Uyehara	Shirt		6	Dinner Table
9	111	2	Mercedez Uyehara	Cell Phone		7	Home Theater

Congratulations! You have your first exercise completed correctly.

ANOTHER EXERCISE
(chapter3ex2.xlsx)

You need to create a code finder, in other words, cell A1 will enter a product code and Cell B1 should show the name of the product. In this case you do not have to drag the formulas because you only need a cell that serves as a search engine.

	A	B
1	10	
2		
3	**ID**	**PRODUCT**
4	1	cheese
5	2	chicken
6	3	catfish
7	4	dumplings
8	5	donuts
9	6	eggs
10	7	apples
11	8	avacado
12	9	alfalfa
13	10	lobster
14	11	Lamb
15	12	ketchup

Step 1: Identify the cell in which you will write the formula. Where do you want the result? In **B1**

Step 2: Identify the Lookup Value. The code is what you will use so the Lookup Value will be cell **A1**

Step 3: Identify the Table Array (the database). You will not need to "immobilize" the Table Array because you do not have to drag the formula. The Table Array is **A3:B15**

Step 4: Identify in which column of your Table Array the name of the product is found. The column **2**

Step 5: Choose exact match for the fourth argument: **0**

Step 6: Your formula looks like this:

=VLOOKUP(A1,A3:B15,2,0)

	A	B		A	B
1	10	Lobster	1	4	Dumplings
2			2		
3	**ID**	**PRODUCT**	3	**ID**	**PRODUCT**
4	1	Cheese	4	1	Cheese
5	2	Chicken	5	2	Chicken
6	3	Catfish	6	3	Catfish
7	4	Dumplings	7	4	Dumplings
8	5	Donuts	8	5	Donuts
9	6	Eggs	9	6	Eggs
10	7	Apples	10	7	Apples
11	8	Avacado	11	8	Avacado
12	9	Alfalfa	12	9	Alfalfa
13	10	Lobster	13	10	Lobster
14	11	Lamb	14	11	Lamb
15	12	Ketchup	15	12	Ketchup

Congratulations! Now you know how to create a code finder!.

ANOTHER EXERCISE
(chapter3ex3.xlsx)

Now you will have to do this exercise by yourself. What you are asked to do is to add the names of the employees that made the sales. Remember to look back at the steps in the previous exercise because they are the same, you only need to change the position and arguments of the formula.

	A	B	C	D	E	F	G	H	I	
1			DAILY SALES				PRODUCTS			EMPLOYEES
2	EMPLOYEE ID	PRODUCT ID	EMPLOYEE NAME	PRODUCT DESCRIPTION		ID	DESCRIPTION		ID	NAME
3	111	4		Jeans		1	Shirt		110	Rafugia Sawicki
4	110	5		Watch		2	Cell Phone		111	Mercedez Uyehara
5	110	1		Shirt		3	TV		112	Lavenia Ebner
6	113	3		TV		4	Jeans		113	Janel Joplin
7	112	1		Shirt		5	Watch		114	Soon Daubert
8	111	1		Shirt		6	Dinner Table		115	Myles Probst
9	111	2		Cell Phone		7	Home Theater		116	Otto Ridenour
10										

TIP:

In the last worksheet of each exercise you will find the ANSWER KEY.

If you have any doubts you can find the right answers there.

	A	B	C	D	E	F	
1			DAILY SALES				PRODUC
2	EMPLOYEE ID	PRODUCT ID	EMPLOYEE NAME	PRODUCT DESCRIPTION		ID	DESCR
3	111	4		Jeans		1	SI
4	110	5		Watch		2	Cell I
5	110	1		Shirt		3	·
6	113	3		TV		4	Je
7	112	1		Shirt		5	W.
8	111	1		Shirt		6	Dinne
9	111	2		Cell Phone		7	Home
10							
11	TIPS:						
12	Yellow is where you have to write the formula						
13	Green are your Lookup Values						
14	Blue is your Table Array						
15	You can take a look at the answer key if you need						
16							
17							
18							
19							

EXCERCISE | ANSWER KEY | +

¡MORE EXERCISES!

Remember to **download the .xlsx files** that have the exercises for you to practice. The exercises in this chapter are: Chapter3Ex1 to Chapter3Ex7.

QUICK CHAPTER SUMMARY:

- The first step to use Vlookup is always to identify where you will write the formula.

- The second step is to find a Lookup Value that can be related to the database.

- Immobilizing the formula with absolute references will avoid most #N/A errors.

- If you have any doubts, you can go to the Answer Key of the exercise.

Are you enjoying this book?

Do you think it's easy to understand?

Have the exercises helped you learn faster?

Without knowing your opinion I won't know if the book has helped you to become a better Vlookup user.

You can share your thoughts with me by simply writing a **Review on Amazon.**

CHAPTER 4

COMMON ERRORS AND HOW TO FIX THEM

WHAT IS AN ERROR?

An error in Excel is a text that **warns you that something in your formula or arguments is incorrect**. Excel tells you the type of Error you are facing so you know how to solve it.

In Vlookup you can usually find 4 types of Errors: #N/A, #REF!, #Value! and #Name!.

#N/A ERROR

What does this one warn?

This error indicates that your formula didn't find the Lookup Value in the Table

Array.

When does it happen?

When the Lookup Value doesn't exist in the first column of the Table Array. It may be because the Table Array points to a range outside the database.

It also occurs when the Lookup Value is slightly different in the database. For example, "id12" without intermediate space is not the same as "id 12" with intermediate space.

In the image you can see the #N/A errors:

The error of "Sylvia Bramee" happens because within the database is written in a different way, as "Sylvia Brame". For that reason Vlookup doesn't "find" it.

The error of Jonh Smith occurs because it doesn't even exist in the database, obviously Vlookup doesn't find it.

	A	B	C	D	E	F
1						
2	NAME	CELL PHONE		EMPLOYEE NAME	CITY	CELL PHONE
3	Sylvia Bramee	#N/A		Markita Przybyla	New York	(289) 715-4821
4	Tesha Mooney	(883) 549-8918		Delilah Ridge	Los Angeles	(579) 903-7287
5	Delilah Ridge	=VLOOKUP(A5;D5:G14,3,0)		Kimbra Fuquay	Chicago	(880) 146-6017
6	Sook Goodpasture	(573) 447-9831		Erlinda Clogston	Houston	(473) 952-3051
7	Markita Przybyla	#N/A		Sylvia Brame	Philadelphia	(294) 217-8826
8	Jonh Smith	#N/A		Mandy Borey	Phoenix	(508) 450-7687
9				Sook Goodpasture	San Antonio	(573) 447-9831
10				Cristin Hogans	San Diego	(524) 313-5936
11				Tesha Mooney	Dallas	(883) 549-8918
12				Eddy Castano	San Jose	(327) 362-2184

The error of Delilah Ridge and Markita Pryzbyla is due to the lack of absolute references, both names are outside the Table Array therefore Vlookup does not find them and returns #N/A.

How to fix it?

Step 1: Confirm that the Lookup value doesn't have spaces at the beginning, middle or end. Remember that for Vlookup to work the Lookup Value must match and be written just like in the database.

Step 2: Check that the Table Array you

chose is correctly positioned in each formula you wrote. Forgetting to use absolute references is the main cause of #N/A.

> **Remember:**
>
> **Forgetting to use the Absolute References in the Table Array is the main cause of #N/A**

#REF! ERROR

What does this one warn?

#REF! Error tells you that within your formula you refer to a cell that is not valid for that formula.

When does it happen?

It happens when you have a written formula, for example **=VLOOKUP(A3,$F$2:$G$9,2,0)** and then you delete a cell that you included in the formula. Suppose you delete column A, by having A3 in the first argument of the formula. In this case the result will show #REF! and if you want to read the formula the error will appear like this **=VLOOKUP(#REF!,$F$2:$G$9,2,0)**

Another reason why #REF! occurs is because a column number that does not exist (within the Table Array) is written in the 3rd argument. For example: If you have **$F$2:$G$9** as Table Array (2 columns), the maximum number in Column Index Number should be 2. With a Table Array of 2 columns and a Column Index Number of 3 you will get a #REF!

	A	B	C	D	E	F
1						
2	**NAME**	**CELL PHONE**		**EMPLOYEE NAME**	**CITY**	**CELL PHONE**
3	Sylvia Brame	#¡REF!		Markita Przybyla	New York	(289) 715-4821
4	Tesha Mooney	(883) 549-8918		Delilah Ridge	Los Angeles	(579) 903-7287
5	Delilah Ridge	(579) 903-7287		Kimbra Fuquay	Chicago	(880) 146-6017
6	Sook Goodpasture	(573) 447-9831		Erlinda Clogston	Houston	(473) 952-3051
7	Markita Przybyla	(289) 715-4821		Sylvia Brame	Philadelphia	(294) 217-8826
8				Mandy Borey	Phoenix	(508) 450-7687
9				Sook Goodpasture	San Antonio	(573) 447-9831

Now "Sylvia Brame" is well written, no longer shows #N/A but shows #REF! What's going on?

NAME	CELL PHONE	
Sylvia Brame	=VLOOKUP(A3,D$3:G$12,5,0)	

If we look at the formula we can see that the third argument (Column Index Number) is 5, when the Table Array only contains 4 columns that are D, E, F and G (Column G does not appear in the image because it contains the annual sales that are irrelevant to this example).

Then because column 5 of the Table Array doesn't exist, Excel shows #REF!. The solution is to change the 5 to a 3.

How to solve it?

Step 1: If you deleted any column, row or cell. Modify the formula manually. This is the most common cause. When you shape your spreadsheet, it is common to delete cells, causing the #REF error!

Step 2: Verify that the Column Index Number doesn't exceed the number of columns that the Table Array has.

#VALUE! ERROR

What does this one warn?

Indicates that your formula is wrong and normally the problem is found in the third argument, column index number.

When does it happen?

This error is more common in nested formulas (formulas that contain other formulas within them). In nested formulas it is likely that the value in Column Index Number is 0 or negative. In this case, #VALUE appears.

NAME	CELL PHONE
Sylvia Brame	#¡VALOR!
Tesha Mooney	(883) 549-8918
Delilah Ridge	(579) 903-7287
Sook Goodpasture	(573) 447-9831
Markita Przybyla	(289) 715-4821

Same example with Sylvia Brame, now

she has the error #VALUE! (#VALOR! In Spanish). What's going on?

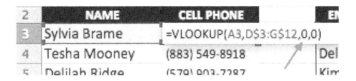

In the third argument, Column Index Number is a 0 instead of a column number.

How to solve it?

Step 1: Directly look at the third argument. Check that it doesn't contain any number of columns greater than the Table Array, no negative number or 0.

#NAME! ERROR

What does this one warn?

The name of your formula is misspelled or an argument that requires a number has text.

When does it happen?

If you write a wrong formula name this error appears. For example if instead of =VLOOKUP you write **=VLOOKUO** or **=VLOOLUP** the result will be the #NAME error.

If in the Column Index Number argument you type Text instead of Numbers you also get the error.

The Range Lookup argument only supports 4 options: TRUE, FALSE, 1 and 0. If you write anything else in that argument you will get the #NAME! Error too.

	NAME	CELL PHONE
1		
2	**NAME**	**CELL PHONE**
3	Sylvia Brame	(294) 217-8826
4	Tesha Mooney	#¿NOMBRE?
5	Delilah Ridge	(579) 903-7287
6	Sook Goodpasture	#¿NOMBRE?
7	Markita Przybyla	#¿NOMBRE?
8		
9	#NAME!	

Now you have 3 #NAME! errors (#NOMBRE! In Spanish). What's going on? The formulas must be revised one by one to discover what happens.

2	**NAME**	**CELL PHONE**
3	Sylvia Brame	(294) 217-8826
4	Tesha Mooney	=VLOOKU(A4,D$3:G$12,3,0)

Tesha Mooney's formula is misspelled, indicating "VLOOKU" instead of "VLOOKUP". That causes the #NAME! error.

5	Delilah Ridge	(579) 903-7287
6	Sook Goodpasture	=VLOOKUP(A6,D$3:G$12,a,0)

Sook's formula has a letter in the Column Index Number argument, that argument only accepts numbers. That causes the #NAME!

6	Sook Goodpasture	#¿NOMBRE?
7	Markita Przybyla	=VLOOKUP(A7,D$3:G$12,3,o)
8		

Markita's formula has a letter within the fourth argument that only accepts 0, 1, TRUE or FALSE. That causes the #NAME!.

How to solve it?

Step 1: Check that your formula is well written.

Step 2: Check the Column Index Number argument, it should only contain numbers.

Step 3: Check the Range Lookup argument, you only have 4 options in that argument.

EXERCISE (chapter4ex1.xlsx)

Now your task is to eliminate the errors of all the VLOOKUP formulas in the following table:

	A	B	C	D	E	F	G	H	I
1									
2	ID	2			ID	AGE	EMPLOYEE NAME	CITY	CELL PHONE	CAR BRAND
3	NAME	#N/A			1	48	Markita Przybyla	New York	(289) 715-4821	Alfa Romeo
4	CELL PHONE	#¡REF!			2	57	Delilah Ridge	Los Angeles	(579) 903-7287	Aston Martin
5	CITY	#¡VALOR!			3	26	Kimbra Fuquay	Chicago	(880) 146-6017	Audi
6	CAR BRAND	#¿NOMBRE?			4	45	Erlinda Clogston	Houston	(473) 952-3051	Bentley

Remember, the main thing to eliminate any error is to ask yourself the following questions:

Question 1: What error is it?

Question 2: Which are the main causes of this error?

Question 3: Which are the main solutions for that error?

The answers to the previous questions have been obtained in this chapter. If you have any questions, you just have to go back and review the steps to solve any of the errors.

In the case of #N/A the problem is found in the Table Array. **You can clearly see that ID 2 is outside the selected Table Array**. This happens very commonly when you drag the VLOOKUP formula and forget to add absolute references ($$) to the Table Array.

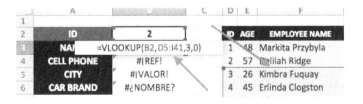

The solution is to extend the Table Array to D3:I41 and add absolute references.

In the case of the #REF error, the problem is found in the Column Index Number argument. The columns of the Table Array are 6 (D, E, F, G, H and I), while the argument indicates 7.

The solution is to change the 7 in Column Index Number to a 5.

In the case of the #VALUE error, the problem is found in the Column Index Number argument that has a 0. Remember that the argument only accepts values greater than 1.

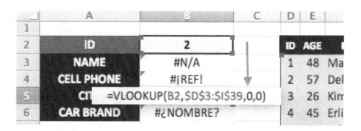

The solution is to change the 0 in Column Index Number to a 4, which is the city column in the Table Array.

In the case of the #NAME error, the problem is found in the name of the formula. It has "VLOKUP" written, which is incorrect. The correct formula is VLOOKUP.

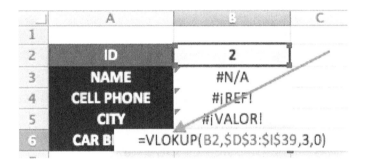

The solution is to change the name of the formula.

The solved exercise looks like this:

MORE EXERCISES

It's time for you to practice with the exercise files to eliminate errors:

Chapter4ex2

Chapter4ex3

Chapter4ex4

Chapter4ex5

QUICK CHAPTER SUMMARY:

- Using Vlookup, there are mainly 4 types of errors
- The first step to solve them is to identify which type of error is
- The second step is to ask: Which are the main causes and the possible solutions for that specific error?

In general, errors occur due to a badly placed Table Array, an incorrect Column Index Number, an error in the name of a formula or lack of a parenthesis.

CHAPTER 5

VLOOKUP TROUGH DIFFERENT WORKSHEETS

WHAT ARE THE WORKSHEETS?

WORKSHEETS are pages from your Excel workbook. Due to the large amount of data that is normally used, the information is organized on different pages called worksheets.

Different worksheets are used to keep the information neater and cleaner. It is a way in which you can visualize only the information that you want at that moment.

You can access each worksheet at the bottom of the spreadsheet, you will find them as small tabs.

	A	B	C	D
1				LAST SALES
2	STORE ID	EMPLOYEE ID	PRODUCT ID	EMPLOYEE NAM
3	1004	111	4	Kum Ayala
4	1002	110	5	Tera Eifert
5	1003	110	1	Ivey Burghardt
6	1006	113	3	Julieann Blick
7	1002	112	1	Kenia Tandy
8	1006	111	1	Frankie Engebrets
9	1006	111	2	Elenora Sarris
10				

SALES | STORES | +

BENEFIT OF USING VLOOKUP TROUGH DIFFERENT WORKSHEETS

You already know that Vlookup can get information from a database (that you specify in your argument Array Table) to make the job easier and faster. But **most of the time the databases are in another worksheet.**

With Vlookup you can bring information from a different worksheet without any problem. One of the advantages of having your database in another worksheet is that you have less visible information and your work looks cleaner and more professional.

If you do not believe me, imagine a database of 20 columns wide and 4,000 rows of information, those are 80,000 cells full of information that you do not want to have in your main worksheet. And in case you ask, yes, I have worked with that amount of data, is visually exhausting.

HOW IS VLOOKUP USED THROUGH WORKSHEETS?

EXERCISE (chapter5ex1.xlsx)

To do this exercise together, open your Excel file and follow my instructions. I'll show you the simplest way to do it.

As always, we have our table that needs to be filled with correct information about the cities where the sales were made. And we also have our database of stores and their cities but it is in another worksheet. What do we do?

	A	B	C	D	E	F
1				LAST SALES		
2	STORE ID	EMPLOYEE ID	PRODUCT ID	EMPLOYEE NAME	PRODUCT DESCRIPTION	CITY
3	1004	111	4	Kum Ayala	Jeans	
4	1002	110	5	Tera Eifert	Watch	
5	1003	110	1	Ivey Burghardt	Shirt	
6	1006	113	3	Julieann Blick	TV	
7	1002	112	1	Kenia Tandy	Shirt	
8	1006	111	1	Frankie Engebretson	Shirt	
9	1006	111	2	Elenora Sarris	Cell Phone	
10						

SALES | STORES | +

	A	B	C	D
1				
2	STORE ID	STATE	CITY	ZIP CODE
3	1001	TEXAS	Houston	91910
4	1002	TEXAS	Dallas	28475
5	1003	TEXAS	Austin	17365
6	1004	CALIFORNIA	Los Angeles	39272
7	1005	CALIFORNIA	San Diego	14421
8	1006	CALIFORNIA	San Francisco	32453
9	1007	FLORIDA	Jacksonville	10373
10	1008	FLORIDA	Miami	60598
11				

SALES | STORES | +

Step 1: Identify in which cell you will write your first formula. As you may have noticed, I always use the first row. In this case, the winning cell is F3.

Step 2: Identify your Lookup Value. Remember to ask yourself, which value I can use that is also in the database? You can notice that Store ID is in the table that we must fill and it is also in our database.

> **In case the Reference Value you want to use is in the middle or to the right of your database, just do the following:**
>
> **1: Insert a column to the left of the database**
>
> **2: Copy the column you want to use as the first column of your Table Array (where your Lookup Value is located)**
>
> **3: Paste it to the left of your database.**

Step 3: Start writing the formula and the first argument.

	A	B	C	D	E	F
1				LAST SALES		
2	STORE ID	EMPLOYEE ID	PRODUCT ID	EMPLOYEE NAME	PRODUCT DESCRIPTION	CITY
3	1004	111	4	Kum Ayala	Jeans	=VLOOKUP(A3,
4	1002	110	5	Tera Eifert	Watch	
5	1003	110	1	Ivey Burghardt	Shirt	

Step 4: When you are about to write the second argument (Table Array) you will need to stop, click on the worksheet where

the database is located and choose the range of your Table Array.

STORE ID	EMPLOYEE ID	PRODUCT ID	EMPLOYEE NAME	PRODUCT DESCRIPTION	CITY
1004	111	4	Kum Ayala	Jeans	=VLOOKUP(A3,
1002	110	5	Tera Eifert	Watch	
1003	110	1	Ivey Burghardt	Shirt	
1006	113	3	Julieann Blick	TV	
1002	112	1	Kenia Tandy	Shirt	
1006	111	1	Frankie Engebretson	Shirt	
1006	111	2	Elenora Sarris	Cell Phone	#1
					CLICK

SALES / STORES +

	255			fx	=VLOOKUP(A3,STORES!A3:D10	
	A	B	C	D	E	F
1						
2	STORE ID	STATE	CITY	ZIP CODE		
3	1001	TEXAS	Houston	91910		
4	1002	TEXAS	Dallas	28475		
5	1003	TEXAS	Austin	17365		
6	1004	CALIFORNIA	Los Angeles	39272		
7	1005	CALIFORNIA	San Diego	14421		#2
8	1006	CALIFORNIA	San Francisco	32453		Select
9	1007	FLORIDA	Jacksonville	10373		table array
10	1008	FLORIDA	Miami	60598		

Did you notice that just before your Table Array the legend Stores appears? That means you're telling Excel to take that argument from the Worksheet called "Stores".

You could manually write in the formula **Stores!** before your Table Array, but it would not allow you to visually count the columns to add the third argument. That's why I recommend that you click on the worksheet of the database to fill the Table Array.

Step 5: Continue with the third and fourth argument of the formula and press Enter to finish it.

The correct result for the first sale, store 1004, is the city of Los Angeles.

			LAST SALES		
1					
2	STORE ID	EMPLOYEE ID	PRODUCT ID	EMPLOYEE NAME	PRODUCT DESCRIPTION	CITY
3	1004	111	4	Kum Ayala	Jeans	Los Angeles
4	1002	110	5	Tera Eifert	Watch	

The complete formula is:

VLOOKUP(A3,STORES!$A$3:$D$10,3,0)

As you can see Vlookup works exactly the same with different worksheets. The only difference is the procedure to add the name of the worksheet together with an exclamation mark **(e.g. Store!)** in the Table Array argument.

MORE EXERCISES

It's time to practice with the exercise files:

Chapter5ex1

Chapter5ex2

Chapter5ex3

Chapter5ex4

QUICK CHAPTER SUMMARY:

- Worksheets help to work in order.
- Vlookup is used the same way through different worksheets

The only difference is that the "Name of the worksheet!" is added.

CHAPTER 6

VLOOKUP FOR DIFFERENT REFERENCE VALUES

Sometimes you don't find any reference value that you can use, in other words, the table you must fill out and your database don't have any value that matches exactly because they are written differently, and still you must relate them.

The goal when that happens is that you are able to create your own reference value to match the database. You have 2 options to do it: Modify the table that you are going to fill or modify your database.

EXERCISE (chapter6ex1.xlsx)

We will solve together the next

exercise. You are asked to relate the 2 tables and get the ZIP code of each store but the database you have (in another worksheet) doesn't have any Lookup Value that you can match exactly.

In a table you must fill in the column "Store", and the stores are numbered (eg 1001, 1002), while in the database the same column "Store" includes the word "Store + ID" (eg Store 1001, Store 1002). Our job is to match them and then use Vlookup.

	A	B	C	
1				LA
2	STORE ID	EMPLOYEE ID	PRODUCT ID	EN
3	1004	111	4	Kum
4	1002	110	5	Tera
5	1003	110	1	Ivey
6	1006	113	3	Julic
7	1002	112	1	Ken
8	1006	111	1	Fran
9	1006	111	2	Eler

	A	B
1		
2	STORE ID	STAT
3	Store 1001	TEXAS
4	Store 1002	TEXAS
5	Store 1003	TEXAS
6	Store 1004	CALIFOR
7	Store 1005	CALIFOR
8	Store 1006	CALIFOR
9	Store 1007	FLORIDA
10	Store 1008	FLORIDA

Step 1: Identify the Lookup Value you will use. In the absence of an exact Lookup Value you should use the most similar and make modifications.

Step 2: Choose the modification that best suits you

Option 1: You can modify the table that you must fill by ADDING the word "Store" and a space " " before each store ID. For this, follow the steps below.

Step 2.1.1: Insert 1 Column to the left of your table. To do so, click on Column A (right in the letter A) and the whole column will be selected, now press Ctrl followed by the + sign to insert the column.

Step 2.1.2: Write the following formula = _"Store "&B3_ and drag the formula down.

What does that formula mean? It tells Excel that you want to write what is in quotes, "Store " (note the space I'm leaving at the end), and then put that together (**&** is the symbol that is used to connect) with the data in B3. **This way you get the value you are looking for "Store 1001", which matches your database.**

Step 2.1.3: Drag the formula to add "Store " to all stores so you can use VLOOKUP now that you already have 2 values that match exactly.

	A	B STORE ID	C EMPLOY ID
1			
2			
3	Store 1004	1004	111
4	Store 1002	1002	110
5	Store 1003	1003	110
6	Store 1006	1006	113
7	Store 1002	1002	112
8	Store 1006	1006	111
9	Store 1006	1006	111

**Option 2:** You can modify the Database by DELETING the word "Store"

and the space to match your table. In other words, just leave the store ID without the "Store" word.

Step 2.2.1: To do this, go to your database and **select all the cells from which you want to delete the word "Store".**

Step 2.2.2: Press **Ctrl + F**, it will open a window named "Find and Replace"

Step 2.2.3: Select the **Replace** option. In the first field you need to write "Store " without quotes **(be sure to write the word and a space at the end).**

Step 2.2.4: Leave empty the **"Replace with"** field to tell Excel that you want to replace "Store" with nothing. In other words, that tells Excel that you want to delete what you indicated in the first field.

Step 2.2.5: Select **"Replace all"**, and that's it. You have your IDs that now match your table exactly.

Step 3: Either of the options you have chosen allows you to have a Reference Value that matches exactly. Now you can use Vlookup as you already know.

MORE EXERCISES

It's time to practice, the files are:

Chapter6ex1

Chapter6ex2

QUICK CHAPTER SUMMARY:

- You can create your own "unique" reference value to match the database
- You can join words or cells using the **&** symbol

- You can delete a repetitive word in the database using Ctrl + F and the "Replace With" option.

CHAPTER 7

VLOOKUP WHEN YOU NEED RESULTS OF MULTIPLE CELLS

Sometimes you can't control the shape of databases, sometimes they are downloaded directly from the company's ERP system, that's why you should be prepared for different scenarios.

Now you are presented with a scenario where your database has employees from different stores and from different cities. Each employee has their own identification number within the company and you need to create a search engine that when someone writes the employee's ID, it shows the full name and the city, all in a single cell. The disadvantage is that your database gives you the information in different columns, even the first and last names are in separate columns.

In such a situation, where there are many names, cities and repeated states (in general, when there is repeated data), you must create your **Unique Result.**

> **The objective in this situation is to create a new column, combining several columns, so that your result is accurate and unique.**

EXERCISE (chapter7ex1)

You already know the scenario. You have a database with ID, First Name, Last Name, City and State. You must create a search engine where when you write the ID of each employee **the result shows the Name, Last Name and City at the same time.**

	A	B	C	D
1	**ID**	**NAME AND CITY**		.
2				
3	**ID**	**NAME**	**LAST NAME**	**CITY**
4	1	John	Smith	Houston
5	2	Marvin	Tegeler	Houston
6	3	Gertrude	Koester	Philadelphia
7	4	Herta	Crinklaw	Phoenix
8	5	Quintin	Blank	San Antonio
9	6	Blake	Sills	San Diego
10	7	Jamie	Husbands	Dallas
11	8	Gracie	Studstill	San Jose
12	9	Wenona	Rocchio	Austin
13	10	Conchita	Benford	Indianapolis
14	11	Becki	Davalos	Jacksonville

What to do? It's easy, use **&** to join values in a new column.

Step 1: In a column to the right of your database, add the "Full Name" header in F3. Just to add a name to that column

Step 2: Now you need to join (concatenate) the necessary data using the **&** symbol. The formula you write in F4 would be the following:

$$=B4\&" "\&C4\&","\&" "\&D4$$

Pay attention to the details and you will notice that I added spaces in quotes and also a comma. If we divide the formula to explain it is easier, this is what you tell Excel with each part:

• **= B4&" "** write what is in B4 and merge it with a blank

• **&C4** then join B4 and space with C4

• **&","** then joins B4, space and C4 with a comma.

• **&" "** then joins B4, the space, C4 and the comma with another space

• **&D4** finally adds what is in D4 to all of the above.

So you get B4, a space, C4, a comma, a space and D4. In this case the formula would show the result: **John Smith, Houston**.

Step 3: Drag the formula down to merge all the data and voila, you have a new column (F) that can give you the result you want.

Step 4: Use the Vlookup formula as you already know. Use Column Index Number as the column you just created.

> **You must enhance your creativity and learn other Excel formulas to be able to offer solutions in different scenarios.**

MORE EXERCISES

It's time to practice with the exercise files:

Chapter7ex1

Chapter7ex2

Chapter7ex3

QUICK CHAPTER SUMMARY:

- The **&** symbol is used to concatenate (join) text or different cells

- Like the formulas the symbol **=** is used at the beginning
- **" "** is used to create spaces
- If you need to join a specific text you need to add it in quotation marks (e.g. **= "Employee "&B4**)

If you need to join the text of two cells you do not need to add quotes (e.g. **=B3&B4**).

CHAPTER 8

VLOOKUP AND FUNCTION "IF"

To recap quickly, so far you have learned the benefits of the Vlookup formula, its arguments and how it works. You have also learned what the absolute references are, the Vlookup errors and their main causes, how to use Vlookup in different worksheets and even how to separate or join values to create a unique Lookup Value and a Unique Result.

Now it's time for you to become a Level 2 Vlookup Champion and learn to use nested functions.

WHAT IS A NESTED FUNCTION?

A nested function **is a function INSIDE**

another function. In other words, a formula is an argument of another function. Is that possible? It is, and in fact it is very convenient because you can do automate processes.

> **Nested functions help make processes more automatic but require learning how to use several functions at the same time.**

In this book we will use Vlookup as an argument of another function or we will use another function as one of the four arguments of Vlokup.

WHAT IS THE "IF" FUNCTION AND WHICH ARE ITS ARGUMENTS?

It's time to learn the new function: "IF". It is a logical function that performs the following:

1. Perform a logical test that we indicate

2. If the logical test is true, it returns a result

3. If the logical test is false, it returns another result.

For example, imagine that you want the function to write "approved" and "failed" depending on the grade obtained in an exam, if it is less than or equal to 59 means failed, if it is greater than or equal to 60 means approved.

The first argument of the "IF" function is the logical test. On it you have to write any condition you want to be fulfilled. Some of the conditions that you can include are these:

• **C4=C5** Equality between cells

• **C4=12** Equality of a cell with a particular value

• **C4="OK"** Equality of a cell with a particular word (The word must be inside quotes)

• **C4<10** The cell is less than the value 10

• **C4>10** The cell is greater than the value 10

The second argument of the IF

function is the value if the logical test is true. In other words, if the logical test is fulfilled, then the IF function writes the word found in the second argument as the result.

The third argument is the value that is shown when the logical test is false. If the logical test is not met, the function writes the third argument.

IF function structure is:

=IF(logical test, value if test is true, value test is if false)

Then the function in the students' example would be:

IF=(C3<=59,"passed","failed")

The trick to "read" the structure of the IF function is to read it as follows:

If C3 is less than or equal to 59 then write "passed", IF it is not, then write "failed"

The above statement has helped me understand any IF function, including nested functions.

> IF is the formula in English.
>
> If you use Excel in Spanish, the formula works the same, with the only difference that IF in Spanish is called SI.
>
> You only need to write in the formula =SI instead of =IF and voila, everything else remains the same.

THE "IF" FUNCTION AND THE VLOOKUP FUNCTION TOGETHER

The IF and Vlookup functions can be used together (nested) to make searches a bit more automatic. If we talk about nesting those two functions, the most common way is to use a function IF and INSIDE it you add the Vlookup function.

> **Vlookup can be "nested" in any of the 3 arguments of the IF function.**

This form of nesting is used when you want Excel to search for a value (with Vlookup) as long as a logical test is performed beforehand (analyzed by the IF function).

For example, if you wanted to search in a database only when a certain cell (e.g. B2) contains the word "search", you would use the logical test of the IF function:

- In the first argument you would write:

=IF($B$2 ="Search"

Remember to immobilize with absolute references $$

- In the second argument you would write the Vlookup function as you know it. This process is called nesting a function within another function.

- In the third argument you would write

what you want to have as a result in case **B2** does not contain the word **"Search"**. The third argument could be **"You have not ordered me to search"**, or any phrase that comes to your mind.

EXERCISE (chapter8ex1)

Let's solve an exercise together. You have two student databases, one with current grades and another with payment status.

You need to fill the table that you have on the left side with Vlookup but you are asked something different from the previous occasions: **The table should show the payment status when Cell B1 contains the word "payment". If cell B2 is empty then the table should show the grades.**

	A	B	C	D	E	F	G
1	CODE			←			
2							
3		STUDENT	RESULT		STUDENT	GRADES	PAYMENT STATUS
4		Mercedez Uyehara			Gerard Dubin	92	PAID
5		Lovie Semmes			Refugia Sawicki	73	OVERDUE
6		Willia Stallings			Mercedez Uyehara	41	PAID
7		Bradly Schwindt			Lavenia Ebner	54	PAID
8		Mariette Benesh			Janel Joplin	42	PAID
9		Elton Bubb			Soon Daubert	69	OVERDUE
10					Myles Probst	90	PAID
11					Otto Ridenour	64	PAID

A very useful trick to facilitate the process of nesting a formula is to advance step by step through each of the arguments. Remember that in a nested formula each argument will be another formula.

In this case, the first argument will be the logical test, the second argument will be a VLookup function that will show the status of the payments (if the logical test is fulfilled) and the third argument will be ANOTHER Vlookup function that would show the grades (if the logical test is not met)

Step 1: Select cell C4 to start modifying the formula by double clicking and start writing the IF function.

The logical test of the IF function would be $B$2="payment", therefore the first function argument would look like this:

=IF($B$1="payment",

	A	B	C	D
1	CODE			
2				
3		STUDENT	RESULT	ST
4		Mercedez Uyehara	=IF($B$1="payment"	
5		Lovie Semmes		Refugia
6		Willia Stallings		Mercer

Step 2: Now you need to write the second IF argument, which will be the VLOOKUP NESTED function. That is, in the second IF argument, the four VLOOKUP arguments will be included.

The formula now continues like this:

=IF($B$1="payment",VLOOKUP(B4,$E$4:$G$32,3,0),

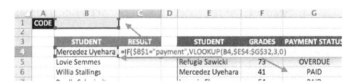

That means that if **B1 contains the word "payment" Excel will use in that cell the formula:**

VLOOKUP=(B4,$E$4:$G$32,3,0)

And the result will be what you find in column 3 of the Table Array **$E$4:$G$32** (the payment status). But what happens if B1 does not contain the word "payment"? Let's go to step 3.

Step 3: If B1 does not contain the word "payment" the formula must give you as a result the grade of the student. That VLOOKUP formula (the one that seeks the grades) is the one that must be nested in the third argument.

The complete formula looks like this:

=IF($B$1="payment",VLOOKUP(B4,E 4:$G$32,3,0),VLOOKUP(B4,$E$4:$G$32,3 ,0))

The formula means the following:

- **=IF($B$1="payment",** If B1 has "Payment" word
- **VLOOKUP(B4,$E$4:$G$32,3,0)** Uses Vlookup to obtain the 3rd column (payment status) from the database

- **VLOOKUP(B4,$E$4:$G$32,3,0)** If B1 doesn't have "Payment" it uses Vlookup to obtain the 2nd column (grades) from the database.

NOTE: Note that there is a double closing of parentheses at the end **))** because the first one is the closing of the second VLOOKUP formula and the second one is the closing of the IF formula completely.

Step 4: Drag the formula

	A	B	C
1	CODE		
2			
3		STUDENT	RESULT
4		Mercedez Uyehara	41
5		Lovie Semmes	30
6		Willia Stallings	100
7		Bradly Schwindt	54
8		Mariette Benesh	59
9		Elton Bubb	77

	A	B	C
1	CODE	payment	
2			
3		STUDENT	RESULT
4		Mercedez Uyehara	PAID
5		Lovie Semmes	PAID
6		Willia Stallings	PAID
7		Bradly Schwindt	PAID
8		Mariette Benesh	PAID
9		Elton Bubb	PAID

MORE EXERCISES

It's time to practice with the exercise files:

Chapter8ex1

Chapter8ex2

QUICK CHAPTER SUMMARY:

- Nested functions are functions that take the place of an argument within another function. They are a function within another function.

- The IF function is a condition. If the condition is met a result is obtained, if the condition is not met another result is obtained.

- The possible results of the IF function can be preset results (e.g. "Failed", "Approved") or nested formulas (e.g. SUM, VLOOKUP).

CHAPTER 9

VLOOKUP AND THE "IFERROR" FUNCTION

WHAT IS "IFERROR"?

Do you remember the ERRORS we talked about in Chapter 4? **There is a function with which you can decide what result you want in case you get an error. That function is called IFERROR.**

For example, you can order Excel to perform a search with Vlookup and at the same time indicate that in case the result is an ERROR Excel must write "YOU NEED TO CHECK YOUR FORMULA". That way instead of getting an error in your result (e.g. #N/A) you would get the text you want.

IFERROR is the formula in English.

If you use Excel in Spanish, the formula works the same, with the only difference that **IFERROR** in Spanish is called **SI.ERROR.**

You only need to write in the formula **=SI.ERROR** instead of **=IFERROR** and voila, everything else remains the same.

ADVANTAGES AND DISADVANTAGES OF THE IFERROR FUNCTION

The main advantage of the function is that you can control the result in case of error. You can even decide that Excel must not write anything in case of error, so you can leave the cell blank. That is achieved by writing 2 quotes together in the second argument of IFERROR.

Another advantage of IFERROR is

that you can NEST another function in your arguments, that way you can say:

"Excel, I want you to execute this formula, but if that formula produces an error I want you to execute this OTHER formula."

The disadvantage of the IFERROR function is that, as you probably already realized, it doesn't show the type of error that the formula has (e.g. you do not know if it is #N/A, #REF!, #VALUE! OR #NAME!) Then if you want to fix the error it would be a bit more difficult.

But, after all, if you use IFERROR it's because you already know that you don't want to see any ugly errors on your Excel sheet, don't you think?

IFERROR FUNCTION ARGUMENTS

You have only two arguments in this function: Value and Value if error. Pretty simple.

• **Value:** It is the main function. The function you want to perform. Normally this is where VLOOKUP is nested, in the first argument.

• **Value if error:** This is what you will get in case the function in the "Value" argument results in an error. You have two options:

1) A fixed value (e.g. "Review", "You made a mistake", etc.)

2) Other formula, for example: Sum, IF, another Vlookup function looking in another database or any other formula you want .

So, in a simple way: **The first argument is what you want to calculate. The second argument is what you want Excel to write or calculate if something goes wrong in the first argument.**

The structure of the function is:

=IFERROR(Value you want, Value in case of error)

It is time to start with the exercises nesting Vlookup inside IFERROR.

EXERCISE OF VLOOKUP + IFERROR (chapter9ex1.xlsx)

Let's solve this exercise together. In the following exercise you are presented with another scenario of students. You are a teacher and you have a list of the students that will take your classes this course, but you want to know their grades from the last course to have an idea of the type of students they are (although anyone can have a bad grade from time to time or)

The principal of the school has last year's student lists but you will give classes to students who are new to the school and don't appear on last year's lists. In this case the Vlookup formula will show you the error #N/A. How will you solve it? Let's do the exercise

Step 1: Analyze the scenario. You will notice that the Vlookup formula is the one you need to use. So proceed to write it and fill the grades of all the students.

Write the following formula in C3 and drag it to get the students' grades:

VLOOKUP(B3,$E$3:$F$31,2,0)

Step 2: Surprise! We have three ugly #N/A errors. We can't leave those mistakes there and there is no way to fix the formula because in fact the formula is correctly written.

The problem is that these students "didn't exist last year", they are new and there is no way they can appear in your search. Analyzing the scenario, it is necessary to insert an IFERROR formula to avoid those #N/A.

	A	B	C	D	E	F
1						
2		STUDENT	RESULT		STUDENT	LAST YEAR GRADES
3		Mercedez Uyehara	41		Gerard Dubin	92
4		John Smith	#N/A		Refugia Sawicki	73
5		Willia Stallings	100		Mercedez Uyehara	41
6		Martin Johnson	#N/A		Lavenia Ebner	54
7		Mariette Benesh	59		Janel Joplin	42
8		Elton Bubb	77		Soon Daubert	69
9		Lovie Semmes	30		Myles Probst	90
10		Bradly Schwindt	54		Otto Ridenour	64
11		Ben Ramsey	#N/A		Margot Shults	91
12					Nery Ambler	66
13					Coleman Lamkin	35

Step 3: You must use the formula IFERROR and within it you need to nest the formula VLOOKUP. Start by writing the formula in C3

=IFERROR(

Step 4: Now write the first IFERROR argument. Remember that the first argument is "the result you want to get" or "the formula you want to execute". In this case, **you must nest VLOOKUP in the first argument:**

=IFERROR(VLOOKUP(B3,$E$3:$F$31,2 ,0),

	A	B	C	D	E
1					
2		STUDENT	RESULT		STUDENT
3		=IFERROR(VLOOKUP(B3,$E$3:$F$31,2,0),			
4		John Smith			Refugia Sawicki
5		Willia Stallings			Mercedez Uyehara

That means that as a first option, cell C3 will use

VLOOKUP(B3,$E$3:$F$31,2,0).

But what happens if the formula results in the #N/A error?

Step 5: The second IFERROR argument is "the result you want to get in case the first argument (VLOOKUP) causes an error". In other words, with the second argument of IFERROR you order Excel what you want it to write automatically in case of finding an error. I want you to write "New Students".

To do that the formula would be this:

=IFERROR(VLOOKUP(B3,$E$3:$F$31,2,0),"New Students")

This means that **C3** will execute VLOOKUP and show the result of column 2 of the Table Array **$E$3:$F$31**, *BUT IF THIS RESULTS IN AN ERROR*, then Excel will write "New Students".

Step 6: Now just drag the formula from

C3 to C11 to get the results.

	A	B	C	D	E	F
1						
2		**STUDENT**	**RESULT**		**STUDENT**	**LAST YEAR GRADES**
3		Mercedez Uyehara	41		Gerard Dubin	92
4		John Smith	New Students		Refugia Sawicki	73
5		Willia Stallings	100		Mercedez Uyehara	41
6		Martin Johnson	New Students		Lavenia Ebner	54
7		Mariette Benesh	59		Janel Joplin	42
8		Elton Bubb	77		Soon Daubert	69
9		Lovie Semmes	30		Myles Probst	90
10		Bradly Schwindt	54		Otto Ridenour	64
11		Ben Ramsey	New Students		Margot Shults	91
12					Nery Ambler	66
13					Coleman Lamkin	35

Congratulations! Now you know how to use IFERROR + VLOOKUP.

MORE EXERCISES

It's time to practice with the exercise files:

Chapter9ex1

Chapter9ex2

QUICK CHAPTER SUMMARY:

- The IFERROR function is used to decide what you want to be written in that cell in case of an Error.
- It only has two very easy arguments.
- The first argument has (nested) the formula you want to execute.
- The second argument indicates what you want to write in case the first argument results in an error.

CHAPTER 10

INDEX AND MATCH.
VLOOKUP ALTERNATIVE TO SERCH
FROM RIGHT TO LEFT

Do you remember that Vlookup can only show results that are to the right of the Lookup Value? There is a solution for that: Two functions called INDEX and MATCH.

Let me warn you something before moving on with this chapter. Maybe this is the longest chapter in the whole book because you need to perfectly master a function (MATCH) before you can use its nested version (INDEX + MATCH). It is not difficult, but you will need some practice to feel comfortable with this nested function.

These two functions have a lot of

flexibility when searching, with the disadvantage that they are a bit more complex to learn and use than Vlookup, but they are completely necessary when you look for values to the left of the Lookup Value.

The main difficulty of this nested function (INDEX + MATCH) is that you will need a Range for INDEX and a Range for MATCH (although most of the times you will need 2 ranges for MATCH). Which means that in the same formula you will have 3 different ranges. Remember this as you progress through this chapter.

MATCH FUNCTION

The MATCH function searches within a range, looking for the word that you indicate. The range MUST be of several rows and ONE single column, or of several columns and ONE single row. This is because the MATCH function shows a number as a result, the position where the word you indicated is found.

◢	A	B	C	D	E
1	CAT 1	BEAR 2	DOG 3	BULL 4	**3**
2					

In the example image we have a range **A1:D1** (one row and four columns) and we are looking for the word "DOG" that is in C1. The function shows as result 3. Why? Because **A1 is position 1, B1 is position 2, C1 is position 3 and D1 is position 4.**

When the range is horizontal, **MATCH** counts the positions from left to right.

MATCH is the formula in English.

If you use Excel in Spanish, the formula works the same, with the only difference that **MATCH** in Spanish is called **COINCIDIR.**

Here I show you another example:

◢	A	B	C	D	E	F
1	4	1	2	3	4	5
2		PEN	PENCIL	PRINTER	LAPTOP	DESK

The range is B2:F2 (one row, five columns). We are searching for the word "LAPTOP" found in E2. The MATCH function shows the value 4 as a result. Why? **B2 is the position 1, C2 the position 2, D2 the position 3, E2 the position 4 and F2 the position 5.**

> **When the range is vertical, MATCH counts the positions from top to bottom**

In the previous examples it is easy to find the position of the word, but imagine when you have a list of hundreds of values, knowing the MATCH function can save you a lot of time.

MATCH STRUCTURE

The syntax (structure) of MATCH is as follows:

=MATCH(Lookup Value, Table Array, Match Type)

Lookup Value: You and I also know it as a reference value. It is the value you are looking for, the value of which you want to find its position and it can be text (e.g. "LAPTOP") or it can be a cell (e.g. in A1 the word "LAPTOP" is found, so the Lookup Value you set is A1).

Table Array: It is the Range where MATCH will search. Remember that it must be a range of 1 column and several rows or of 1 row and several columns.

Match Type: 0 is exact match and 1 is approximate match. Just as Vlookup.

MATCH EXERCISE (chapter10ex1.xlsx)

Now we will solve a little Match exercise together to make sure you have learned it.

You have a vertical food list and you need to find the position of "CROUTONS" within the range

	A
1	CROUTONS
2	
3	
4	Bard
5	Kahlua
6	Provolone
7	Powdered Sugar
8	Gouda
9	Chicken
10	Irish Cream Liqueur
11	Amaretto
12	Mayonnaise
13	Rhubarb
14	Ginger
15	Croutons
16	Peanut Butter

Step 1: Identify your Lookup Value, in this case it is A1.

Step 2: Write the following formula in A2:

=MATCH(A1,A4:A16,0)

Why A1? Because it will look for the word Croutons

Where will it look for it? In the range A4:A16

Is it an exact match? Yes, that's why the third argument is 0

What result will it show? 12

Why 12? Well, it's a vertical range. **A4 is position 1, A5 is position 2 and so on, so if you keep counting you will find that A15 is position 12.**

	A
1	CROUTONS
2	=MATCH(A1,A4:A16,0)
3	
4	Bard
5	Kahlua
6	Provolone
7	Powdered Sugar
8	Gouda
9	Chicken
10	Irish Cream Liqueur
11	Amaretto
12	Mayonnaise
13	Rhubarb
14	Ginger
15	Croutons
16	Peanut Butter
17	

Make sure you solve the other exercises within the same chapter10ex1.xlsx file. Why? Because the INDEX function that I am going to show you needs the MATCH function NESTED. In other words, your result in INDEX will depend on your mastery of MATCH.

INDEX FUNCTION

The INDEX function is used in 99% of the cases together with MATCH. That is why it is necessary that at this moment you master MATCH, if you have not completed the previous exercises I recommend that you stop and complete them to ensure that you know how to use MATCH.

INDEX is the formula in English.

If you use Excel in Spanish, the formula works the same, with the only difference that INDEX in Spanish is called INDICE.

The INDEX function is used to obtain a result that "matches" the column number and row number that you indicate. In other words, you select a range (imagine that the range is A1:F10), then you use INDEX to find the value in row 5 of the range and column 3. INDEX shows you the result.

	A	B	C	D	E	columns G
1	$252	$ 867	$ 202	$ 29	$ 985	$232
2	$858	$ 408	$ 1	$128	$ 458	$380
3	$420	$ 662	$ 770	$ 11	$ 59	$232
4	$521	$ 390	$ 925	$ 32	$ 854	$186
5	$515	$ 658	$ 587	$185	$ 443	$120
6	$526	$ 335	$ 357	$265	$ 790	$125
7	$554	$ 114	$ 733	$ 55	$ 593	$194
8	$656	$ 132	$ 680	$770	$ 498	$357
9	$523	$ 377	$ 735	$139	$ 541	$564
10 rows						
11		587	INDEX		INDEX	458
12		ROW 5 and COLUMN 3			ROW 2 and COLUMN 5	

The result of the INDEX corresponds to row 5 of the range and column 3. Why? INDEX counts the rows from top to bottom and the columns from left to right.

The result of cell **B11 (587)** corresponds to row number 5 (from top to bottom) and to column 3 (from left to right).

The result of cell **F11 (458)** corresponds to row number 2 (from top to bottom) and to column 5 (from left to right).

But there is no point in manually adding the row number and the column number because you would have to do the manual search. This is where MATCH comes in with its ability to find positions within a range.

INDEX STRUCTURE

The structure of the INDEX function is the following:

=INDEX(Array, Row Number, Column Number)

Array: It is the range where the function will search. The range can have any number of rows and any number of columns.

Row Number: It is the number of the row counting from top to bottom. Within the range chosen in Array, the row above would be number 1, the next row below would be number 2, and so on.

Column Number: It is the number of the column counting from left to right. Within the range chosen in Array, the first column on the left would be number 1, the next column on the right would be number 2, and so on.

> **INDEX shows as a result the value found at the intersection of the row number, and the column number.**

INDEX EXERCISE (chapter10ex2.xlsx)

In this example you have a range **(B2:G10),** and you need INDEX to show the value of E3. The formula would be the following:

=INDEX(B2:G10,2,4)

	A	B	C	D	E	F	G
1							
2		$2,770	$ 3,051	$ 3,252	$3,062	$ 965	$2,922
3		$2,128	$ 3,349	$ 2,300	$1,608	$2,280	$4,406
4		$4,606	$ 4,822	$ 4,754	$3,572	$4,549	$3,998
5		$2,835	$ 2,063	$ 486	$4,353	$1,551	$ 571
6		$ 115	$ 4,485	$ 3,711	$1,600	$2,852	$ 864
7		$4,054	$ 4,242	$ 1,456	$4,058	$3,677	$4,146
8		$1,216	$ 662	$ 4,189	$3,034	$3,212	$4,101
9		$1,076	$ 2,235	$ 1,930	$2,334	$2,504	$ 388
10		$ 276	$ 2,207	$ 1,244	$3,466	$ 200	$2,185

Why B2:G10? Because it is the range where you want to find the data

Why 2 in the second argument? E3 is in the second row (top to bottom) of the selected range.

Why 4 in the third argument? E3 is in the fourth column (from right to left) of the selected range.

This is how you the exercise is solved and the formula that should be used in this case.

	A	B	C	D	E	F	G
1							
2		$2,770	$ 3,051	$ 3,252	$3,062	$ 965	$2,922
3		$2,128	$ 3,349	$ 2,300	$1,608	$2,280	$4,406
4		$4,606	$ 4,822	$ 4,754	$3,572	$4,549	$3,998
5		$2,835	$ 2,063	$ 486	$4,353	$1,551	$ 571
6		$ 115	$ 4,485	$ 3,711	$1,600	$2,852	$ 864
7		$4,054	$ 4,242	$ 1,456	$4,058	$3,677	$4,146
8		$1,216	$ 662	$ 4,189	$3,034	$3,212	$4,101
9		$1,076	$ 2,235	$ 1,930	$2,334	$2,504	$ 388
10		$ 276	$ 2,207	$ 1,244	$3,466	$ 200	$2,185
11							
12		=INDEX(B2:G10,2,4)					

Let's practice again. In the same exercise and the same range. Which would be the formula to find the result of B4?

The formula is **=INDEX(B2:G10,3,1)** Why? B4 is in the third row and in the first column.

	A	B	C	D	E	F	G
1							
2		$2,770	$ 3,051	$ 3,252	$ 3,062	$ 965	$2,922
3		$2,128	$ 3,349	$ 2,300	$ 1,608	$2,280	$4,406
4		$4,606	$ 4,822	$ 4,754	$ 3,572	$4,549	$3,998
5		$2,835	$ 2,063	$ 486	$ 4,353	$1,551	$ 571
6		$ 115	$ 4,485	$ 3,711	$ 1,600	$2,852	$ 864
7		$4,054	$ 4,242	$ 1,456	$ 4,058	$3,677	$4,146
8		$1,216	$ 662	$ 4,189	$ 3,034	$3,212	$4,101
9		$1,076	$ 2,235	$ 1,930	$ 2,334	$2,504	$ 388
10		$ 276	$ 2,207	$ 1,244	$ 3,466	$ 200	$2,185
11							
12			$ 1,608		=INDEX(B2:G10,3,1)		

MORE INDEX EXERCISES

Now it is your turn to practice with what remains of the exercise **chapter10ex2** and with the exercise **chapter10ex3**.

INDEX + MATCH EXERCISE (chapter10ex4.xlsx)

Now we come to the important phase of INDEX and MATCH. We will use the two functions at the same time solving an exercise together. It is important that at this point you already know how to use nested functions and that you have solved the Vlookup + IF and Vlookup + IFERROR exercises.

You have a scenario where the last few year sales of several employees are shown. It is necessary to create a tool that shows the sales amount when you write the name and the year.

The main difference in this table is that the names of the employees (Lookup Values) are on the right side of the table, and the results (sales) are on the left side. With a table like this it is impossible to use Vlookup.

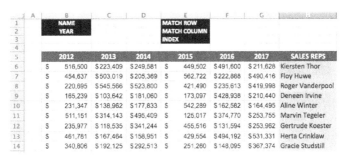

With the "results" on the left (sales) of the lookup value (name) you realize that you need to use the INDEX + MATCH functions.

INDEX + MATCH (WITHOUT NESTED FORMULA)

The first option (and the simplest one) is to solve the exercise with each formula separately, that way you can see and understand the process.

Step 1: Write the MATCH formula for the "Match Row" field. This formula will show the row number of the name that we write in the "Name" field. In other words, the cell with the name will be the Lookup Value. The formula would be:

$$=MATCH(C1,H6:H14,0)$$

Why that formula? MATCH will look for the name that is in C1 within the range **H6:H14**. In this case Floy Huwe is the position number 2 from top to bottom.

Step 2: Write the MATCH formula for the "Match Column" field. This formula will show the column number of the year that we write in the "Year" field. In other words, the cell with the Year will be the Lookup Value. The formula would be:

$$=MATCH(C1,B5:G5,0)$$

	B	C	D	E	F	G
	NAME	FLOY HUWE		MATCH ROW	2	
	YEAR	2015	←	MAT	=MATCH(C2,B5:G5,0)	
				INDEX		
	2012	2013	2014	2015	2016	2017
S	516,500	S 223,409	S 249,581	S 449,502	S 491,600	S 211,628 Kie
S	454,637	S 503,019	S 205,369	S 562,722	S 222,888	S 490,416 Flc

Why that formula? Because MATCH will look for the year written in C2 within the range **B5:G5** and will show the horizontal position in which it is. In this case 2015 is position number 4.

Step 3: Now you must use INDEX function with the previous MATCH results. For the second argument (Row Number) you will use the result of Match Row (the names) and for the third argument (Column number) you will use the result of Match Column (the years). The formula would be the following:

$$=INDEX(B6:G14,F1,F2)$$

	B		C		D		E		F		G	H
	NAME	FLOY HUWE				**MATCH ROW**		2				
	YEAR	2015				**MATCH COLUMN**		4				
						INDE	=INDEX(B6:G14,F1,F2)					
	2012		**2013**		**2014**		**2015**		**2016**		**2017**	**SALES REP**
$	516,500	$	223,409	$	249,581	$	449,502	$	491,600	$	211,628	Kiersten Thor
$	454,637	$	503,019	$	205,369	$	562,722	$	222,888	$	490,416	Floy Huwe
$	220,695	$	545,566	$	523,800	$	421,490	$	235,613	$	419,998	Roger Vander

Why? INDEX function will search within Table Array B6:G14. And what will it look for? It will look for the result that is in row 2 (which matches the name FLOY HUWE) and in column 4 (which coincides with Year 2015).

The result is $ 562,722.

INDEX + MATCH EXERCISE (WITH NESTED FORMULA) chapter10ex5.xlsx

Now we will carry out the same exercise together but without using so many intermediate steps. We will create the nested formula from the beginning and the process will be shorter. It is possible that the explanation is a bit longer, but once you understand it you will see that it is very easy to nest Match within Index.

Step 1: You will start by writing the

formula INDEX and its first argument, which is the range of possible results. The formula would look like this with the first argument.

$$=INDEX(B6:G14,$$

	A	B	C	D	E	F	G	H
1		**NAME**	FLOY HUWE		**INDE**	=INDEX(B6:G14,		
2		**YEAR**	2015					
3								
4								
5		**2012**	**2013**	**2014**	**2015**	**2016**	**2017**	**SALES REPS**
6		$ 516,500	$ 223,409	$ 249,581	$ 449,502	$ 491,600	$ 211,628	Kiersten Thor
7		$ 454,637	$ 503,019	$ 205,369	$ 562,722	$ 222,888	$ 490,416	Floy Huwe
8		$ 220,695	$ 545,566	$ 523,800	$ 421,490	$ 235,613	$ 419,998	Roger Vanderpool
9		$ 165,239	$ 103,642	$ 181,060	$ 173,097	$ 428,938	$ 210,440	Deneen Irvine
10		$ 231,347	$ 138,962	$ 177,833	$ 542,289	$ 162,582	$ 164,495	Aline Winter
11		$ 511,151	$ 314,143	$ 495,409	$ 125,017	$ 374,770	$ 253,755	Marvin Tegeler
12		$ 235,977	$ 118,535	$ 341,244	$ 455,516	$ 131,594	$ 253,962	Gertrude Koester
13		$ 461,781	$ 167,464	$ 158,951	$ 429,554	$ 494,192	$ 531,331	Herta Crinklaw
14		$ 340,806	$ 192,125	$ 292,513	$ 251,260	$ 148,095	$ 367,374	Gracie Studstill

Why does the Array (range) only cover Sales and doesn't cover years or names? Because in the next steps we will use a different range for MATCH that will range from H6 (Kiersten Thor) to H14 (Gracie Studstill). So, **Kiersten Thor will be the position 1 of MATCH, which will coincide with the first row of the INDEX range.**

Always try to have the first row of your MATCH range matching the first row of the INDEX Array

Step 2: Add the nested MATCH function that indicates the row number. To make it easier, the 3 MATCH arguments must be within the second INDEX argument. The formula now looks like this:

=INDEX(B6:G14,MATCH(C1,H6:H14,0),

	B	C	D	E	F	G	H
1	**NAME**	FLOY HUWE		**INDE**	=INDEX(B6:G14,MATCH(C1,H6:H14,0),		
2	**YEAR**	2015					
3							
4							
5	**2012**	**2013**	**2014**	**2015**	**2016**	**2017**	**SALES REPS**
6	$ 516,500	$ 223,409	$249,581	$ 449,502	$ 491,600	$211,628	Kiersten Thor
7	$ 454,637	$ 503,019	$205,369	$ 562,722	$ 222,888	$490,416	Floy Huwe
8	$ 220,695	$ 545,566	$523,800	$ 421,490	$ 235,613	$419,998	Roger Vanderpool
9	$ 165,239	$ 103,642	$181,060	$ 173,097	$ 428,938	$210,440	Deneen Irvine
10	$ 231,347	$ 138,962	$177,833	$ 542,289	$ 162,582	$164,495	Aline Winter
11	$ 511,151	$ 314,143	$495,409	$ 125,017	$ 374,770	$253,755	Marvin Tegeler
12	$ 235,977	$ 118,535	$341,244	$ 455,516	$ 131,594	$253,962	Gertrude Koester
13	$ 461,781	$ 167,464	$158,951	$ 429,554	$ 494,192	$531,331	Herta Crinklaw
14	$ 340,806	$ 192,125	$292,513	$ 251,260	$ 148,095	$367,374	Gracie Studstill

Why? Because MATCH will look for the value that is in C1 (Floy Huwe) within the range **H6:H14**, with exact match (0 in third argument) and the result will be the row number in which it is. Floy Huwe is in row # 2 of the range, counting from top to bottom because it is a vertical range.

The result of Index's second argument will be 2 (just like the previous exercise), although the formula still needs to be completed.

Step 3: For the third argument of INDEX the same has to be done as in the second argument, with the only difference that now the value sought will be the year. The complete formula is the following:

=INDEX(B6:G14,MATCH(C1,H6:H14,0), MATCH(C2,B5:G5,0))

	A	B	C	D	E	F	G	H
1		**NAME**	FLOY HUWE		=INDEX(B6:G14,MATCH(C1,H6:H14,0),MATCH(C2,B5:G5,0))			
2		**YEAR**	2015					
3								
4								
5		**2012**	**2013**	**2014**	**2015**	**2016**	**2017**	**SALES REPS**
6		$ 516,500	$ 223,409	$249,581	$ 449,502	$ 491,800	$ 211,628	Kiersten Thor
7		$ 454,637	$ 503,019	$205,369	$ 562,722	$ 222,888	$ 490,416	Floy Huwe
8		$ 220,695	$ 545,566	$523,800	$ 421,490	$ 235,613	$ 419,998	Roger Vanderpool
9		$ 165,239	$ 103,642	$181,060	$ 173,097	$ 428,938	$ 210,440	Deneen Irvine
10		$ 231,347	$ 138,962	$177,833	$ 542,289	$ 162,582	$ 164,495	Aline Winter
11		$ 511,151	$ 314,143	$495,409	$ 125,017	$ 374,770	$ 253,755	Marvin Tegeler
12		$ 235,977	$ 118,535	$341,244	$ 455,516	$ 131,594	$ 253,962	Gertrude Koester
13		$ 461,781	$ 167,464	$158,951	$ 429,554	$ 494,192	$ 531,331	Herta Crinklaw
14		$ 340,806	$ 192,125	$292,513	$ 251,260	$ 148,095	$ 367,374	Gracie Studstill

Why? Because MATCH will look for the year written in C2 within the range B5:G5 and will show the position in which it is from left to right. In this case, 2015 is in position 4 of the MATCH range, so the third INDEX argument will be 4.

Step 4: The result is $ 562,722. Same as last exercise, but everything was done in just one nested formula.

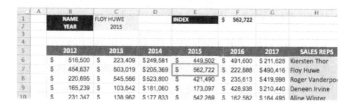

	A	B	C	D	E	F	G	H
1		**NAME**	FLOY HUWE		**INDEX**	$ 562,722		
2		**YEAR**	2015					
3								
4								
5		**2012**	**2013**	**2014**	**2015**	**2016**	**2017**	**SALES REPS**
6		$ 516,500	$ 223,409	$249,581	$ 449,502	$ 491,600	$211,628	Kiersten Thor
7		$ 454,637	$ 503,019	$205,369	$ 562,722	$ 222,888	$490,416	Floy Huwe
8		$ 220,695	$ 545,566	$523,800	$ 421,490	$ 235,613	$419,998	Roger Vanderpo
9		$ 165,239	$ 103,642	$181,060	$ 173,097	$ 428,938	$210,440	Deneen Irvine
10		$ 231,347	$ 138,962	$177,833	$ 542,269	$ 162,582	$164,495	Aline Winter

You can now change the names and the years and you will see that in all cases you get the correct result.

Congratulations! Now you know how to use an alternative to VLOOKUP when your Lookup Values are to the right of the database.

QUICK CHAPTER SUMMARY:

- The VLOOKUP function can't be used to search from right to left.
- To do that it is necessary to use the INDEX + MATCH functions
- MATCH shows the position of a searched value within a vertical or horizontal range.

- INDEX shows the desired value within a range, as long as you indicate in which row and in which column it is.

CHAPTER 11

QUICK FINAL TIPS

This book wouldn't be complete without a series of final recommendations that can help you to be not only a Vlookup Champion, but also an Excel Champion.

Here (in this short chapter) I can't teach you everything I'm going to recommend because they are extensive topics that would not fit in a few pages, it is also information that I teach deeply in other Excel Champions books.

However want to make you the following recommendations with the hope that you recognize the main tools that you must learn to be an Excel Champion.

WHY DO YOU NEED TO LEARN KEYBOARD SHORTCUTS?

First of all I want to recommend that you learn Excel keyboard shortcuts. Keyboard shortcuts are the easiest and fastest way to increase your productivity in Excel. You can easily cut your work time in half.

The reality is that there are more than 100 keyboard shortcuts. My recommendation is that you learn the 10 or 20 main ones. Which are the main ones? The ones you use the most depending the kind of work you have to do in Excel.

Some of those that everybody should use are:

Ctrl + C to copy a cell (with format too)

Ctrl + V to paste the cell that you copied

Ctrl + X to cut the cell (instead of copying it, you remove it from its cell to paste it in another cell)

Ctrl + to insert a column or row (selecting the column or row previously)

Ctrl - to delete a column or row (selecting the column or row previously)

Surely with these shortcuts you can move a little faster. But there are more that are quite useful.

WHY DO YOU NEED TO LEARN CONDITIONAL FORMATTING?

You will agree that the human eye identifies faster the colors and shapes than numbers. For the same reason, traffic lights have colors instead of numbers or words.

The conditional formatting in Excel is used to add colors or shapes when certain conditions are met, making the data user-friendly and giving the opportunity to recognize patterns within the data.

Imagine for a moment that you have a table with 100 data and you need to find the values that are closest to the average.

Option 1: The first option is to use the AVERAGE function and then manually search for those values within the table.

Option 2: The fastest and easiest option is to use Conditional Format so that Excel automatically colors the data that is closest to the average, and that's it, you'll have the data you need highlighted in the color you want in a few seconds, it doesn't matter if your table has 100, 1000 or 10000 numbers.

If you would like to search for the 10 highest values within a table, you can do so. If you would like to focus only on data that is less than the average, you can color them automatically. If you want to identify the data that are between 2 values, you can do it in less than 30 seconds.

That is why I recommend conditional formatting. Becoming a Conditional Formatting Champion will allow you to find the most relevant information.

WHY DO YOU NEED TO LEARN

MORE FUNCTIONS?

There are hundreds of functions that can help you to better perform your work, however you may not know them. Sometimes a new function that you learn can save you hours of weekly work in the office.

The important thing to remember about functions is that they tend to relate to each other and become stronger tools when combined or in the form of nested formulas.

I'll give you an example you already know: VLOOKUP. The VLOOKUP function is quite strong and useful on its own, but when you learned to use IF together with VLOOKUP, three things happened:

1) You learned a new function: VLOOKUP

2) You learned a new function: IF

3) You learned a new tool: IF + VLOOKUP

When you learn just two functions you actually have three tools in your toolbox. That is, your tools are not just the number of functions you master, but also include the combinations you can make between those functions.

So the more functions you know, the more combinations you can make and the more chances you have to become an Excel Champion.

WHY DO YOU NEED TO LEARN TO USE CHARTS?

Charts are, by excellence, the way to communicate quantitative information in the business world, in non-profit organizations, in schools, in governmental organizations, in health areas, in sports, etc.

It's very simple, if you want to effectively communicate your numerical data, you need to master the Excel Charts. That includes the use of tables and the correct positioning of them, the selection of the data that you need, the Chart Type selection and the modification of the parameters of the chart.

Additionally it becomes necessary that you learn to discover what a chart wants to "tell you". Correctly analyzing the data in a chart usually leads to better decisions.

If you want to make better decisions in your job or company, it is very likely that becoming an Excel Charts and Graphs Champion will benefit you.

I WOULD LOVE TO READ YOUR COMMENTS

Before you leave I would like to tell you Thank You for buying my book. It is my wish that the information you obtained in Excel VLOOKUP Champion helps you in your job or business, and that you can have greater productivity and more free time to use it in the activities that you like the most.

I realize that you could have chosen among several other Excel books but you chose Excel VLOOKUP Champion and you invested your time and effort. I am honored to have the opportunity to help you.

I'd like to ask you a small favor. **Could you take a minute or two and leave a Review**

of Excel **VLOOKUP** Champion on Amazon?

This feedback will be very appreciated and will help me continue to write more courses that help you and a lot more people.

Share your comments with me and other readers by visiting this link:

www.bit.ly/vlookupreview1

ABOUT THE AUTHOR

Henry E. Mejia is an online entrepreneur who discovered the great benefits of knowing how to use Microsoft Excel at an advanced level, and now he devotes part of his time to creating courses (books and videos) so that more people can enjoy free time and better opportunities that an Advanced Excel user can have.

Henry also realized that the vast majority of people give away a lot of their life in front of the computer. That time could be used in more productive or more enjoyable activities, only if people knew how to use Excel a little better.

The goal of Henry's books is to open the door for workers and business owners to use Excel more efficiently, so they can have more and better growth opportunities.

Made in the USA
Monee, IL
10 June 2024

59693968R00079